# 50 Farm-Fresh Egg Recipes for Home

By: Kelly Johnson

# Table of Contents

- Classic Scrambled Eggs
- Poached Eggs on Toast
- Deviled Eggs
- Quiche Lorraine
- Shakshuka
- Omelette with Mushrooms and Cheese
- Egg Salad Sandwich
- Huevos Rancheros
- Spanish Tortilla
- Cloud Eggs
- Egg and Avocado Breakfast Bowl
- Baked Avocado Eggs
- Eggplant and Egg Casserole
- Soft-Boiled Eggs with Soldiers
- Bacon and Egg Muffins
- Croque Madame
- Frittata with Spinach and Feta
- Egg Drop Soup
- Breakfast Burrito with Scrambled Eggs
- Veggie Egg Muffins
- Coddled Eggs
- Sunny-Side-Up Eggs with Roasted Tomatoes
- Bacon-Wrapped Eggs
- Sweet Potato and Egg Breakfast Skillet
- Asparagus and Poached Egg Salad
- Eggs Benedict
- Scotch Eggs
- French Toast with Egg and Cinnamon
- Korean Kimchi Egg Stir-Fry
- Egg and Cheese Breakfast Tacos
- Zucchini and Egg Scramble
- Egg Fried Rice
- Mediterranean Eggplant and Egg Bake
- Frittata with Roasted Vegetables
- Smoked Salmon and Scrambled Eggs

- Avocado and Poached Eggs on Toast
- Spinach and Mushroom Egg Cups
- Egg and Chorizo Breakfast Tacos
- Indian-style Masala Eggs
- Breakfast Egg Cups with Ham
- Egg and Bacon Croissants
- Egg Bhurji (Indian-style Scrambled Eggs)
- Lemon Ricotta Pancakes with Poached Eggs
- Quinoa and Eggs Breakfast Bowl
- Bacon, Egg, and Cheese Sandwich
- Poached Eggs with Hollandaise Sauce
- Egg and Spinach Pockets
- Thai Basil Egg Stir-Fry
- Broccoli and Cheddar Egg Bake
- Caramelized Onion and Goat Cheese Omelette

## Classic Scrambled Eggs

**Ingredients:**

- 4 large eggs
- 2 tbsp butter
- Salt and pepper to taste
- Fresh herbs (optional)

**Instructions:**

1. Crack the eggs into a bowl, season with a pinch of salt and pepper, and whisk until well combined.
2. Heat butter in a non-stick pan over medium-low heat.
3. Pour in the eggs and let them cook undisturbed for a few moments. Stir gently with a spatula, pushing the eggs from the edges towards the center.
4. Continue to cook, stirring occasionally, until the eggs are soft and slightly runny. Remove from heat just before they're fully set for creamy scrambled eggs.
5. Garnish with fresh herbs, if desired, and serve immediately.

**Poached Eggs on Toast**

**Ingredients:**

- 2 eggs
- 2 slices of bread (your choice)
- 1 tbsp vinegar
- Salt and pepper to taste
- Fresh herbs (optional)

**Instructions:**

1. Bring a pot of water to a gentle simmer. Add vinegar to the water (this helps the eggs hold their shape).
2. Crack each egg into a small bowl. Gently slide the eggs into the simmering water.
3. Cook the eggs for 3-4 minutes for soft yolks or longer for firmer eggs. Remove with a slotted spoon.
4. Toast the bread slices and place them on plates.
5. Carefully place poached eggs on top of the toast, season with salt and pepper, and garnish with fresh herbs if desired.

**Deviled Eggs**

**Ingredients:**

- 6 hard-boiled eggs, peeled
- 3 tbsp mayonnaise
- 1 tsp mustard
- 1 tsp vinegar
- Salt and pepper to taste
- Paprika (optional)

**Instructions:**

1. Slice the boiled eggs in half lengthwise and scoop out the yolks into a bowl.
2. Mash the yolks with mayonnaise, mustard, vinegar, salt, and pepper until smooth.
3. Spoon or pipe the filling back into the egg whites.
4. Sprinkle with paprika for garnish and serve chilled.

**Quiche Lorraine**

**Ingredients:**

- 1 pie crust (store-bought or homemade)
- 6 large eggs
- 1 cup heavy cream or milk
- 1 cup cooked bacon, crumbled
- 1/2 cup shredded Swiss cheese
- Salt and pepper to taste
- Fresh parsley (optional)

**Instructions:**

1. Preheat the oven to 375°F (190°C). Place the pie crust in a tart pan and bake for 10 minutes to pre-bake.
2. In a bowl, whisk together eggs, cream (or milk), salt, and pepper.
3. Add crumbled bacon and shredded cheese into the egg mixture and stir to combine.
4. Pour the mixture into the pre-baked crust and bake for 30-35 minutes, or until the quiche is set and golden brown.
5. Allow to cool slightly, garnish with fresh parsley, and serve.

## Shakshuka

### Ingredients:

- 2 tbsp olive oil
- 1 onion, chopped
- 1 bell pepper, chopped
- 2 cloves garlic, minced
- 1 can (14 oz) diced tomatoes
- 1 tsp cumin
- 1/2 tsp paprika
- 4 large eggs
- Salt and pepper to taste
- Fresh cilantro (optional)

### Instructions:

1. Heat olive oil in a large skillet over medium heat. Add the onion and bell pepper and sauté until soft, about 5 minutes.
2. Add garlic, cumin, and paprika, cooking for another minute.
3. Pour in the diced tomatoes with their juices, season with salt and pepper, and simmer for 10-15 minutes until the sauce thickens.
4. Make small wells in the sauce and crack the eggs into the wells. Cover and cook for 6-8 minutes until the eggs are set.
5. Garnish with fresh cilantro and serve with crusty bread.

## Omelette with Mushrooms and Cheese

### Ingredients:

- 3 large eggs
- 1 tbsp butter
- 1/4 cup mushrooms, sliced
- 1/4 cup shredded cheese (cheddar, Swiss, or your choice)
- Salt and pepper to taste

### Instructions:

1. Beat the eggs in a bowl and season with salt and pepper.
2. Heat butter in a non-stick pan over medium heat and sauté mushrooms until softened.
3. Pour the beaten eggs into the pan and cook for 2-3 minutes until the edges begin to set.
4. Add cheese to one half of the omelette and fold it over.
5. Cook for another 1-2 minutes, or until the cheese is melted and the omelette is cooked through.
6. Serve immediately.

**Egg Salad Sandwich**

**Ingredients:**

- 4 hard-boiled eggs, chopped
- 1/4 cup mayonnaise
- 1 tsp Dijon mustard
- 1 tbsp chopped fresh dill or chives
- Salt and pepper to taste
- 2 slices of bread (your choice)

**Instructions:**

1. In a bowl, mix the chopped eggs, mayonnaise, mustard, fresh herbs, salt, and pepper.
2. Spread the egg salad mixture onto a slice of bread.
3. Top with another slice of bread to form a sandwich.
4. Serve immediately or chill before serving.

## Huevos Rancheros

### Ingredients:

- 2 large eggs
- 1 cup salsa (store-bought or homemade)
- 2 corn tortillas
- 1/4 cup refried beans (optional)
- 1/4 cup grated cheese (cheddar, mozzarella, or your choice)
- Fresh cilantro for garnish
- Salt and pepper to taste

### Instructions:

1. Heat the salsa in a small pan and simmer until warmed through.
2. Heat the tortillas in a dry skillet for 1-2 minutes on each side.
3. If using, spread a layer of refried beans on the tortillas.
4. Fry the eggs in a separate pan to your liking (sunny side up or over-easy).
5. Place the eggs on top of the tortillas, spoon salsa over the eggs, and sprinkle with cheese.
6. Garnish with fresh cilantro, salt, and pepper.
7. Serve with extra salsa or avocado on the side.

## Spanish Tortilla

**Ingredients:**

- 4 large eggs
- 2 medium potatoes, thinly sliced
- 1 small onion, thinly sliced
- 1/4 cup olive oil
- Salt and pepper to taste

**Instructions:**

1. Heat olive oil in a large skillet over medium heat. Add potatoes and onions and cook for 10-12 minutes, stirring occasionally, until softened.
2. Beat the eggs in a bowl and season with salt and pepper.
3. Pour the eggs over the potatoes and onions, making sure they are evenly coated.
4. Cook over low heat for 5-7 minutes, until the edges set, then carefully flip the tortilla using a plate or lid and cook the other side for 3-4 minutes.
5. Let cool slightly, then slice and serve warm or at room temperature.

## Cloud Eggs

**Ingredients:**

- 2 large eggs
- Salt and pepper to taste
- Fresh herbs (optional)

**Instructions:**

1. Preheat the oven to 375°F (190°C) and line a baking sheet with parchment paper.
2. Separate the egg whites from the yolks, placing the whites in a large mixing bowl and the yolks in separate small bowls.
3. Beat the egg whites until stiff peaks form, then gently spoon the egg whites onto the baking sheet, creating little nests.
4. Use a spoon to make a small indentation in the center of each egg white mound.
5. Carefully place a yolk into each nest, season with salt and pepper, and bake for 3-5 minutes, or until the yolk is cooked to your preference.
6. Garnish with fresh herbs, if desired, and serve immediately.

## Egg and Avocado Breakfast Bowl

### Ingredients:

- 2 large eggs
- 1 avocado, sliced
- 1/4 cup cherry tomatoes, halved
- 1 tbsp olive oil
- Salt and pepper to taste
- Fresh herbs (optional)

### Instructions:

1. Cook the eggs according to your preference (fried, poached, scrambled, or soft-boiled).
2. While the eggs cook, prepare the other ingredients: slice the avocado and halve the cherry tomatoes.
3. Drizzle olive oil over a bowl, and add the avocado and tomatoes.
4. Top with the cooked eggs and season with salt, pepper, and fresh herbs, if desired.
5. Serve immediately for a nutritious and filling breakfast.

## Baked Avocado Eggs

### Ingredients:

- 2 ripe avocados
- 4 small eggs
- Salt and pepper to taste
- Red pepper flakes (optional)
- Fresh herbs (optional)

### Instructions:

1. Preheat the oven to 375°F (190°C).
2. Cut the avocados in half and remove the pits. Scoop out a little extra flesh to create space for the eggs.
3. Place the avocado halves in a baking dish, ensuring they are stable.
4. Crack one egg into the center of each avocado half.
5. Season with salt, pepper, and optional red pepper flakes.
6. Bake for 12-15 minutes, or until the egg whites are set.
7. Garnish with fresh herbs, if desired, and serve immediately.

## Eggplant and Egg Casserole

### Ingredients:

- 1 large eggplant, sliced into rounds
- 4 large eggs
- 1 cup ricotta cheese
- 1/4 cup grated Parmesan cheese
- 1/4 cup fresh basil, chopped
- Salt and pepper to taste
- Olive oil for greasing

### Instructions:

1. Preheat the oven to 375°F (190°C) and grease a baking dish with olive oil.
2. Layer the eggplant slices in the baking dish, and season with salt and pepper.
3. In a separate bowl, whisk together the eggs, ricotta cheese, Parmesan, and basil.
4. Pour the egg mixture over the eggplant slices and bake for 20-25 minutes, or until the eggs are set.
5. Serve warm as a savory and satisfying breakfast or lunch.

## Soft-Boiled Eggs with Soldiers

### Ingredients:

- 2 large eggs
- 2 slices of bread (your choice)
- Butter (optional)
- Salt and pepper to taste

### Instructions:

1. Bring a small pot of water to a boil and gently lower the eggs into the water.
2. Reduce the heat and simmer for 4-5 minutes for soft-boiled eggs with runny yolks.
3. While the eggs cook, toast the bread and cut it into strips, known as "soldiers."
4. Once the eggs are done, remove them from the water and peel the shells.
5. Serve the eggs with the soldiers for dipping, and season with salt and pepper.

## Bacon and Egg Muffins

### Ingredients:

- 6 large eggs
- 6 slices bacon
- 1/2 cup shredded cheese (cheddar or your choice)
- Salt and pepper to taste
- Fresh herbs (optional)

### Instructions:

1. Preheat the oven to 375°F (190°C) and grease a muffin tin.
2. Line each muffin cup with a slice of bacon, wrapping it around the edges.
3. Crack an egg into each muffin cup.
4. Sprinkle shredded cheese over each egg and season with salt and pepper.
5. Bake for 12-15 minutes, or until the eggs are set and the bacon is crispy.
6. Garnish with fresh herbs and serve immediately.

## Croque Madame

### Ingredients:

- 2 slices of bread
- 2 slices ham
- 1/2 cup grated Gruyère cheese
- 1 tbsp Dijon mustard
- 1 tbsp butter
- 1 large egg
- Salt and pepper to taste

### Instructions:

1. Preheat the oven to 375°F (190°C).
2. Spread Dijon mustard on one side of each slice of bread.
3. Layer one slice of ham and cheese on each piece of bread.
4. Top with the second slice of bread to form a sandwich.
5. In a skillet, melt butter over medium heat and cook the sandwich on both sides until golden brown.
6. Meanwhile, fry an egg in a separate pan to your liking (usually sunny side up).
7. Place the sandwich in the oven for 5 minutes to melt the cheese, then top with the fried egg.
8. Season with salt and pepper, and serve immediately.

# Frittata with Spinach and Feta

## Ingredients:

- 6 large eggs
- 1 cup fresh spinach, chopped
- 1/4 cup crumbled feta cheese
- 1 tbsp olive oil
- Salt and pepper to taste

## Instructions:

1. Preheat the oven to 375°F (190°C).
2. In an oven-safe skillet, heat olive oil over medium heat and sauté the spinach until wilted.
3. In a bowl, whisk together eggs, salt, and pepper.
4. Pour the egg mixture over the spinach and sprinkle with crumbled feta.
5. Cook on the stovetop for 2-3 minutes, then transfer the skillet to the oven.
6. Bake for 10-12 minutes, or until the eggs are set and lightly golden.
7. Let cool for a few minutes before slicing and serving.

## Egg Drop Soup

### Ingredients:

- 4 cups chicken broth (or vegetable broth for vegetarian)
- 2 large eggs
- 1 tsp cornstarch (optional for thicker broth)
- 1 tbsp soy sauce (optional)
- 2 green onions, chopped
- Salt and pepper to taste
- Sesame oil (optional)
- Red pepper flakes (optional)

### Instructions:

1. In a pot, bring the chicken broth to a simmer over medium heat.
2. If using cornstarch, dissolve it in a small amount of cold water and stir into the broth to thicken.
3. Once the broth is simmering, lightly beat the eggs in a bowl.
4. Slowly pour the eggs into the simmering broth while stirring gently to create ribbons of egg.
5. Add soy sauce, salt, and pepper to taste, and continue to simmer for 2-3 minutes.
6. Garnish with chopped green onions, a drizzle of sesame oil, and red pepper flakes (if desired).
7. Serve hot and enjoy.

## Breakfast Burrito with Scrambled Eggs

### Ingredients:

- 2 large eggs
- 1 tortilla
- 1/4 cup shredded cheese (cheddar or your choice)
- 1/4 cup salsa
- 2 tbsp sour cream
- 2 slices cooked bacon or sausage (optional)
- Salt and pepper to taste

### Instructions:

1. Scramble the eggs in a pan over medium heat, seasoning with salt and pepper.
2. Warm the tortilla in a separate pan for a few seconds on each side.
3. Once the eggs are cooked, place them in the center of the tortilla.
4. Top with cheese, salsa, sour cream, and optional bacon or sausage.
5. Roll up the tortilla, folding in the sides to form a burrito.
6. Serve immediately for a delicious breakfast on the go.

**Veggie Egg Muffins**

**Ingredients:**

- 6 large eggs
- 1/4 cup milk
- 1/2 cup diced bell peppers
- 1/4 cup spinach, chopped
- 1/4 cup shredded cheese
- Salt and pepper to taste
- Olive oil for greasing muffin tin

**Instructions:**

1. Preheat the oven to 350°F (175°C) and grease a muffin tin with olive oil.
2. In a mixing bowl, whisk together the eggs, milk, salt, and pepper.
3. Add the diced bell peppers, spinach, and shredded cheese to the egg mixture.
4. Pour the mixture evenly into the muffin tin, filling each cup about 3/4 full.
5. Bake for 15-20 minutes, or until the eggs are set and slightly golden.
6. Let cool for a few minutes before serving.

## Coddled Eggs

### Ingredients:

- 2 large eggs
- Salt and pepper to taste
- Butter (optional)

### Instructions:

1. Fill a small saucepan with water and bring it to a simmer over medium heat.
2. Gently crack the eggs into separate ramekins or small cups.
3. Lower the ramekins into the simmering water, making sure the water covers the eggs by about half.
4. Simmer for 3-4 minutes, or until the egg whites are set but the yolks remain soft.
5. Carefully remove the ramekins from the water and season with salt and pepper.
6. Serve with a dollop of butter or toast if desired.

# Sunny-Side-Up Eggs with Roasted Tomatoes

**Ingredients:**

- 2 large eggs
- 1 cup cherry tomatoes, halved
- Olive oil for roasting
- Salt and pepper to taste
- Fresh herbs (optional)

**Instructions:**

1. Preheat the oven to 375°F (190°C) and toss the halved cherry tomatoes with a little olive oil, salt, and pepper.
2. Spread the tomatoes on a baking sheet and roast for 10-15 minutes, or until soft and slightly caramelized.
3. While the tomatoes are roasting, heat a non-stick skillet over medium heat and crack the eggs into the pan.
4. Cook the eggs without flipping, until the whites are set and the yolks are still runny, about 2-3 minutes.
5. Serve the sunny-side-up eggs with the roasted tomatoes and garnish with fresh herbs, if desired.

## Bacon-Wrapped Eggs

**Ingredients:**

- 4 large eggs
- 4 slices bacon
- Salt and pepper to taste

**Instructions:**

1. Preheat the oven to 400°F (200°C).
2. Wrap each slice of bacon around an individual egg, securing the ends with toothpicks.
3. Place the bacon-wrapped eggs on a baking sheet and bake for 15-20 minutes, or until the bacon is crispy and the eggs are cooked to your desired doneness.
4. Remove the toothpicks and serve with a sprinkle of salt and pepper.

# Sweet Potato and Egg Breakfast Skillet

## Ingredients:

- 1 medium sweet potato, peeled and diced
- 2 large eggs
- 1/4 cup onion, chopped
- 1/4 cup bell pepper, chopped
- Olive oil for sautéing
- Salt and pepper to taste

## Instructions:

1. Heat olive oil in a skillet over medium heat and sauté the onion and bell pepper until softened, about 5 minutes.
2. Add the diced sweet potato to the skillet and cook for another 10 minutes, stirring occasionally, until the sweet potato is tender.
3. Make two small wells in the sweet potato mixture and crack an egg into each well.
4. Cover the skillet and cook for 5-7 minutes, or until the eggs are cooked to your liking.
5. Season with salt and pepper, and serve immediately.

## Asparagus and Poached Egg Salad

**Ingredients:**

- 1 bunch asparagus, trimmed
- 2 large eggs
- Mixed greens (arugula, spinach, etc.)
- Olive oil and lemon for dressing
- Salt and pepper to taste

**Instructions:**

1. Bring a pot of water to a boil and prepare the eggs for poaching by gently cracking them into individual bowls.
2. Trim the tough ends off the asparagus and blanch them in boiling water for 2-3 minutes, until tender but still crisp.
3. Meanwhile, poach the eggs in simmering water for 3-4 minutes, or until the whites are set but the yolks are runny.
4. Assemble the salad by placing mixed greens on a plate, then topping with the asparagus and poached eggs.
5. Drizzle with olive oil, a squeeze of lemon, and season with salt and pepper before serving.

## Eggs Benedict

**Ingredients:**

- 2 English muffins, split
- 4 large eggs
- 1/2 cup hollandaise sauce (store-bought or homemade)
- 4 slices Canadian bacon or ham
- 1 tbsp white vinegar
- Fresh parsley, chopped (for garnish)

**Instructions:**

1. Toast the English muffin halves until golden and crispy.
2. In a skillet, cook the Canadian bacon or ham until lightly browned, then set aside.
3. Fill a saucepan with water and add white vinegar. Bring to a simmer.
4. Crack each egg into a small bowl and gently slide them into the simmering water. Poach for 3-4 minutes, or until the whites are set and the yolks are runny.
5. Place the toasted muffins on plates, then layer each with a slice of cooked bacon or ham.
6. Top with a poached egg, spoon over the hollandaise sauce, and garnish with parsley.
7. Serve immediately.

## Scotch Eggs

**Ingredients:**

- 4 large eggs
- 1 lb ground sausage (or ground turkey)
- 1/2 cup breadcrumbs
- 1/2 tsp salt
- 1/4 tsp black pepper
- 1/2 tsp paprika
- 1/4 tsp garlic powder
- 1/4 tsp onion powder
- 1 egg (for breading)
- Vegetable oil for frying

**Instructions:**

1. Boil the 4 eggs for 7-8 minutes to make them hard-boiled, then peel.
2. In a bowl, mix the ground sausage with breadcrumbs, salt, pepper, paprika, garlic powder, and onion powder.
3. Beat the additional egg in a bowl for breading.
4. Flatten a portion of the sausage mixture in your hand and wrap it around each hard-boiled egg.
5. Dip each sausage-wrapped egg into the beaten egg, then roll in breadcrumbs.
6. Heat vegetable oil in a frying pan over medium heat, then fry the Scotch eggs for about 5-7 minutes, turning to brown on all sides.
7. Drain on paper towels and serve warm.

# French Toast with Egg and Cinnamon

## Ingredients:

- 4 slices of bread (preferably thick-cut)
- 2 large eggs
- 1/2 cup milk
- 1 tsp cinnamon
- 1/2 tsp vanilla extract
- 1 tbsp butter for frying
- Maple syrup for serving

## Instructions:

1. In a bowl, whisk together the eggs, milk, cinnamon, and vanilla extract.
2. Heat a skillet over medium heat and melt the butter.
3. Dip each slice of bread into the egg mixture, coating both sides.
4. Fry the coated bread in the skillet until golden brown on both sides, about 2-3 minutes per side.
5. Serve with maple syrup and a dusting of powdered sugar, if desired.

## Korean Kimchi Egg Stir-Fry

**Ingredients:**

- 2 large eggs
- 1/2 cup kimchi, chopped
- 1 tbsp sesame oil
- 1/4 cup green onions, chopped
- 1/2 tsp soy sauce
- 1/2 tsp gochujang (optional)
- Salt and pepper to taste

**Instructions:**

1. Heat sesame oil in a skillet over medium heat.
2. Add the chopped kimchi and stir-fry for 2-3 minutes until heated through.
3. Push the kimchi to the side and scramble the eggs in the skillet, cooking until scrambled and set.
4. Add soy sauce, gochujang (optional), and season with salt and pepper.
5. Toss everything together and garnish with chopped green onions before serving.

## Egg and Cheese Breakfast Tacos

### Ingredients:

- 4 small tortillas
- 4 large eggs
- 1/2 cup shredded cheese (cheddar, Monterey Jack, or your choice)
- Salsa (optional)
- 1/4 cup avocado, diced (optional)
- Salt and pepper to taste
- 2 tbsp butter for cooking

### Instructions:

1. Scramble the eggs in a bowl and season with salt and pepper.
2. Heat butter in a skillet over medium heat and cook the scrambled eggs until set, about 2-3 minutes.
3. Warm the tortillas in a separate pan for 20 seconds on each side.
4. Fill each tortilla with scrambled eggs and top with cheese, salsa, and avocado.
5. Serve immediately.

## Zucchini and Egg Scramble

### Ingredients:

- 2 large eggs
- 1 zucchini, grated or diced
- 1 tbsp olive oil
- 1/4 cup onion, chopped
- Salt and pepper to taste
- Fresh herbs (optional)

### Instructions:

1. Heat olive oil in a skillet over medium heat and sauté the onion for 2-3 minutes until softened.
2. Add the zucchini and cook for 5-7 minutes until tender.
3. Beat the eggs in a bowl and pour over the cooked zucchini. Scramble until eggs are cooked through.
4. Season with salt and pepper, and garnish with fresh herbs if desired.
5. Serve hot.

# Egg Fried Rice

## Ingredients:

- 2 cups cooked rice (preferably cold)
- 2 large eggs
- 1/2 cup peas and carrots (frozen or fresh)
- 2 tbsp soy sauce
- 1 tbsp sesame oil
- 1/4 cup green onions, chopped
- 1 tbsp vegetable oil for cooking
- Salt and pepper to taste

## Instructions:

1. Heat vegetable oil in a large skillet or wok over medium heat.
2. Scramble the eggs in the skillet, then set them aside.
3. Add sesame oil to the skillet and sauté the peas and carrots until tender, about 5 minutes.
4. Add the rice and soy sauce, and stir-fry for 3-4 minutes.
5. Stir in the scrambled eggs and green onions.
6. Season with salt and pepper, and serve immediately.

## Mediterranean Eggplant and Egg Bake

**Ingredients:**

- 1 large eggplant, sliced into rounds
- 4 large eggs
- 1/2 cup feta cheese, crumbled
- 1/4 cup black olives, sliced
- 1 tbsp olive oil
- 1/2 tsp dried oregano
- Salt and pepper to taste

**Instructions:**

1. Preheat the oven to 375°F (190°C).
2. Heat olive oil in a skillet over medium heat and cook the eggplant slices until tender and lightly browned, about 5 minutes per side.
3. Arrange the cooked eggplant slices in a baking dish.
4. Crack the eggs on top of the eggplant slices, sprinkle with feta cheese, black olives, oregano, salt, and pepper.
5. Bake for 12-15 minutes, or until the eggs are set.
6. Serve hot.

# Frittata with Roasted Vegetables

## Ingredients:

- 6 large eggs
- 1 cup mixed roasted vegetables (such as bell peppers, zucchini, and onions)
- 1/2 cup shredded cheese (optional)
- 2 tbsp olive oil
- Salt and pepper to taste

## Instructions:

1. Preheat the oven to 350°F (175°C).
2. In a bowl, whisk together the eggs, salt, and pepper.
3. Heat olive oil in a skillet over medium heat, add the roasted vegetables, and stir for a few minutes to warm them through.
4. Pour the egg mixture over the vegetables and sprinkle with cheese if desired.
5. Bake in the oven for 10-12 minutes, or until the eggs are fully set.
6. Serve warm.

## Smoked Salmon and Scrambled Eggs

### Ingredients:

- 2 large eggs
- 2 oz smoked salmon, sliced
- 1 tbsp cream cheese (optional)
- 1 tbsp butter for cooking
- Fresh dill or chives (for garnish)
- Salt and pepper to taste

### Instructions:

1. Scramble the eggs in a bowl and season with salt and pepper.
2. Heat butter in a skillet over medium heat, and cook the eggs until they are softly scrambled.
3. Gently fold in the smoked salmon and cream cheese (if using).
4. Garnish with fresh dill or chives and serve immediately.

## Avocado and Poached Eggs on Toast

### Ingredients:

- 2 slices of whole grain or sourdough bread
- 1 ripe avocado, mashed
- 2 large eggs
- 1 tbsp vinegar (for poaching)
- Salt and pepper to taste
- Fresh herbs (optional, for garnish)

### Instructions:

1. Toast the bread slices until crispy and golden.
2. In a saucepan, bring water to a simmer and add vinegar.
3. Crack each egg into a small cup, then gently slide into the simmering water. Poach the eggs for about 3-4 minutes.
4. While the eggs are poaching, mash the avocado and season with salt and pepper.
5. Spread the mashed avocado onto the toasted bread.
6. Once the eggs are poached, place one on each slice of toast.
7. Garnish with fresh herbs, and serve immediately.

## Spinach and Mushroom Egg Cups

### Ingredients:

- 4 large eggs
- 1 cup spinach, chopped
- 1/2 cup mushrooms, diced
- 1/4 cup cheese (cheddar, mozzarella, or your choice)
- 1 tbsp olive oil
- Salt and pepper to taste

### Instructions:

1. Preheat the oven to 375°F (190°C) and grease a muffin tin.
2. In a skillet, heat olive oil over medium heat and sauté the mushrooms until tender, about 5 minutes.
3. Add the spinach to the skillet and cook for another 2 minutes until wilted. Remove from heat and set aside.
4. Spoon the spinach and mushroom mixture into the muffin cups, filling each about halfway.
5. Crack an egg into each cup, then season with salt, pepper, and a sprinkle of cheese.
6. Bake for 12-15 minutes, or until the eggs are set.
7. Let cool slightly before serving.

## Egg and Chorizo Breakfast Tacos

### Ingredients:

- 4 small tortillas
- 4 large eggs
- 1/2 lb chorizo, crumbled
- 1/4 cup cheese (cheddar, Monterey Jack, or your choice)
- Salsa, for serving
- Fresh cilantro, for garnish

### Instructions:

1. Cook the crumbled chorizo in a skillet over medium heat for 5-7 minutes until browned and fully cooked. Remove from heat and set aside.
2. In the same skillet, scramble the eggs until cooked through.
3. Warm the tortillas in a separate pan for about 20 seconds on each side.
4. Fill each tortilla with scrambled eggs and chorizo, then top with cheese, salsa, and fresh cilantro.
5. Serve immediately.

# Indian-style Masala Eggs

## Ingredients:

- 4 large eggs
- 1 onion, chopped
- 1 tomato, chopped
- 2 green chilies, chopped
- 1/4 cup cilantro, chopped
- 1/2 tsp turmeric
- 1 tsp cumin powder
- 1 tsp garam masala
- 1 tbsp oil
- Salt to taste

## Instructions:

1. Heat oil in a skillet over medium heat. Add the chopped onions and cook for 2-3 minutes until softened.
2. Add the chopped tomatoes and cook for 3-4 minutes until softened.
3. Stir in the green chilies, turmeric, cumin powder, garam masala, and salt, then cook for 2 minutes.
4. Crack the eggs directly into the skillet and stir to mix with the masala mixture. Cook until the eggs are scrambled and fully cooked.
5. Garnish with chopped cilantro and serve with naan or rice.

## Breakfast Egg Cups with Ham

**Ingredients:**

- 4 slices of ham
- 4 large eggs
- 1/4 cup shredded cheese (optional)
- Salt and pepper to taste
- Fresh parsley, for garnish

**Instructions:**

1. Preheat the oven to 375°F (190°C) and grease a muffin tin.
2. Place a slice of ham in each muffin cup, forming a cup shape.
3. Crack an egg into each ham cup, then season with salt and pepper.
4. Sprinkle with cheese, if desired.
5. Bake for 12-15 minutes, or until the eggs are set.
6. Garnish with parsley and serve immediately.

## Egg and Bacon Croissants

**Ingredients:**

- 4 croissants
- 4 large eggs
- 8 slices of bacon
- 1/2 cup cheese (cheddar or your choice)
- Salt and pepper to taste

**Instructions:**

1. Preheat the oven to 375°F (190°C).
2. Cook the bacon in a skillet over medium heat until crispy. Remove from heat and set aside.
3. Slice the croissants in half and place on a baking sheet. Toast lightly in the oven for about 5 minutes.
4. In the same skillet, scramble the eggs and season with salt and pepper.
5. Assemble the croissants by layering scrambled eggs, bacon, and cheese.
6. Place back in the oven for 3-5 minutes until the cheese melts.
7. Serve warm.

## Egg Bhurji (Indian-style Scrambled Eggs)

### Ingredients:

- 4 large eggs
- 1 onion, chopped
- 1 tomato, chopped
- 1 green chili, chopped
- 1/4 tsp turmeric
- 1 tsp cumin seeds
- 1/2 tsp garam masala
- 1/4 tsp red chili powder
- 1 tbsp oil
- Fresh cilantro, for garnish
- Salt to taste

### Instructions:

1. Heat oil in a skillet over medium heat. Add cumin seeds and let them splutter.
2. Add the chopped onions and cook for 2-3 minutes until softened.
3. Stir in the tomatoes, green chili, turmeric, garam masala, red chili powder, and salt. Cook for another 3-4 minutes until the tomatoes soften.
4. Crack the eggs into the skillet and stir until scrambled and fully cooked.
5. Garnish with fresh cilantro and serve with bread or chapati.

# Lemon Ricotta Pancakes with Poached Eggs

## Ingredients:

- 1 cup ricotta cheese
- 1 cup flour
- 1 tsp baking powder
- 1/2 cup milk
- 1 large egg
- Zest of 1 lemon
- 1 tbsp lemon juice
- 2 large eggs (for poaching)
- Butter for cooking

## Instructions:

1. In a bowl, combine the ricotta cheese, flour, baking powder, milk, egg, lemon zest, and lemon juice. Mix until smooth.
2. Heat a griddle or skillet over medium heat and melt a little butter.
3. Pour small rounds of batter onto the griddle and cook for 2-3 minutes on each side, until golden brown.
4. Meanwhile, poach the eggs by cracking them into simmering water with a little vinegar. Cook for 3-4 minutes until the whites are set.
5. Serve the pancakes with poached eggs on top, and drizzle with maple syrup.

## Quinoa and Eggs Breakfast Bowl

**Ingredients:**

- 1 cup cooked quinoa
- 2 large eggs
- 1 tbsp olive oil
- 1/4 avocado, sliced
- Fresh herbs (optional)
- Salt and pepper to taste

**Instructions:**

1. Heat olive oil in a skillet over medium heat and cook the eggs to your liking (fried, scrambled, or poached).
2. In a bowl, place the cooked quinoa as the base.
3. Top with the cooked eggs, avocado slices, and any desired fresh herbs.
4. Season with salt and pepper to taste and serve immediately.

## Bacon, Egg, and Cheese Sandwich

**Ingredients:**

- 2 slices of bread (whole grain, sourdough, or your choice)
- 2 large eggs
- 4 slices of bacon
- 2 slices of cheese (cheddar or American)
- Butter for toasting bread
- Salt and pepper to taste

**Instructions:**

1. Cook the bacon in a skillet over medium heat until crispy. Remove and set aside.
2. Toast the bread slices in the skillet with a little butter until golden brown.
3. In the same skillet, cook the eggs to your liking.
4. Assemble the sandwich: place one slice of cheese on each piece of toast, top with the bacon and cooked egg.
5. Close the sandwich and serve warm.

## Poached Eggs with Hollandaise Sauce

### Ingredients:

- 4 large eggs (for poaching)
- 1 tbsp vinegar (for poaching)
- 2 egg yolks
- 1/2 cup unsalted butter, melted
- 1 tbsp lemon juice
- Salt and cayenne pepper to taste

### Instructions:

1. For poached eggs, bring water to a simmer in a saucepan and add vinegar. Crack each egg into a small cup and gently slide them into the water. Cook for 3-4 minutes until the whites are set.
2. To make the hollandaise sauce, whisk egg yolks, melted butter, lemon juice, salt, and cayenne pepper in a bowl until smooth and thick.
3. Serve the poached eggs with a drizzle of hollandaise sauce on top.

## Egg and Spinach Pockets

**Ingredients:**

- 2 large eggs
- 1 cup spinach, chopped
- 2 whole wheat pita pockets or tortillas
- 1/4 cup shredded cheese (optional)
- Salt and pepper to taste

**Instructions:**

1. Scramble the eggs in a skillet over medium heat.
2. Add the chopped spinach to the skillet and cook for 2-3 minutes until wilted.
3. Warm the pita pockets or tortillas in a separate pan.
4. Spoon the scrambled egg and spinach mixture into each pocket, then add shredded cheese if desired.
5. Season with salt and pepper, then serve.

## Thai Basil Egg Stir-Fry

**Ingredients:**

- 2 large eggs, scrambled
- 1 cup cooked rice (preferably day-old)
- 1/2 onion, chopped
- 2 cloves garlic, minced
- 1/4 cup fresh Thai basil leaves
- 1 tbsp soy sauce
- 1 tbsp fish sauce
- 1 tbsp olive oil

**Instructions:**

1. Heat olive oil in a skillet over medium heat. Add the onions and garlic, cooking for 2-3 minutes until softened.
2. Stir in the scrambled eggs and cook until fully set.
3. Add the cooked rice, soy sauce, and fish sauce. Stir well to combine.
4. Add the fresh basil and stir until fragrant.
5. Serve hot, garnished with extra basil if desired.

## Broccoli and Cheddar Egg Bake

**Ingredients:**

- 6 large eggs
- 1 cup broccoli florets, steamed
- 1/2 cup shredded cheddar cheese
- 1/4 cup milk
- Salt and pepper to taste

**Instructions:**

1. Preheat the oven to 375°F (190°C) and grease a baking dish.
2. In a bowl, whisk together eggs, milk, salt, and pepper.
3. Add the steamed broccoli and shredded cheddar cheese to the egg mixture and stir to combine.
4. Pour the mixture into the prepared baking dish and bake for 20-25 minutes, or until set and golden on top.
5. Serve warm, sliced into squares.

# Caramelized Onion and Goat Cheese Omelette

## Ingredients:

- 3 large eggs
- 1/2 onion, thinly sliced
- 2 oz goat cheese, crumbled
- 1 tbsp olive oil
- Salt and pepper to taste

## Instructions:

1. Heat olive oil in a skillet over medium heat and cook the onions for 10-12 minutes, stirring occasionally, until caramelized.
2. Whisk the eggs in a bowl, then pour them into the skillet with the caramelized onions.
3. Cook the eggs until the edges begin to set, then sprinkle goat cheese on top.
4. Fold the omelette in half and cook for another minute until the cheese has melted and the eggs are fully cooked.
5. Serve warm.